I0755973

FINISHING LINE PRESS
www.finishinglinepress.com

Learning How to Drown

poems by

Joseph Kerschbaum

Finishing Line Press
Georgetown, Kentucky

Learning How to Drown

For Valerie and Penny, again and always

ISBN 979-8-89990-363-2 First Edition

ACKNOWLEDGMENTS

The author extends his deepest gratitude to the editors of the following journals where poems from Learning How to Drown first appeared:

Hamilton Stone Review: "Distance to Here"
The Lakeshore Review: "Into Darkness"
Last Stanza Poetry Journal: "Detasseling," "How Ghosts are Born," and "The Past is Never Over"
Of Rust and Glass: "Learning How to Drown"
Trampoline: "People Only Remember the Burning"

Publisher: Leah Huete de Maines
Editor: Christen Kincaid
Cover Art: Vadim Karaska, https://karaska.digitaloriginal.app/artworks/
Author Photo: Annie Prince
Cover Design: Elizabeth Maines McCleavy

Order online: www.finishinglinepress.com
also available on amazon.com

Author inquiries and mail orders:
Finishing Line Press
PO Box 1626
Georgetown, Kentucky 40324
USA

Contents

Into Darkness

At the monolith's base,
I stare upward
in darkness.
From here,
the grain storage silo
extends forever

into the night sky.
I mimic the other kids'
laughter as if
my stomach
isn't churning
or my teeth
aren't chattering.
The wind whispers
with the rasp
of corn husk tongues.
No one else hears

a hushed warning
in the humid air.
This summer,
all the boys proved
their fledgling bravery
by reaching the top.
Except for me. Grasping

the steel bar quiets
my trembling hands.
Muffled cheers erupt
with my first reluctant
step up the rusted ladder.
Is this the rung where
a worker lost their grip

years ago? The echoes
of that incident resonate
as I climb. I concentrate
on placing each unsteady foot
without glancing

downward where blood
was rinsed
out of the gravel.
Generations removed

since the accident,
which some folks insist
is local folklore.
Depends on who you ask.
Everyone has heard
a different name.
None of them

match the tombstones
in the graveyard
on the edge of town.

Detasseling

The field doesn't need a mouth
to swallow you. A wall of mature corn stalks
closes as you enter. It's like you were never

here. Your skin is licked raw by a thousand dry husks.
Blotchy rash of microscopic cuts and relentless sunburn
itches all summer. A breeze whispers

in the swaying tassels overhead. Thrust your hand
above the crops. Your outstretched fingers
look like someone drowning. Mud sucks

at your boot with each step. Remember
your grandparents' advice: lift your heel
with force to snap the soil's grasp.

On your way home, identical cornfields
flank every road. Drive for miles
but feel like you have gone

nowhere. Exhausted, untie your crusted
black laces. Add yours to the row of
muddy boots on the front porch.

The Past is Never Over

"Stop crying and jump!" the floating heads taunt
as they tread neck-deep in the river.

The shivering boy stands at the edge
of the train trestle. His brothers threaten
to climb back up and push him off the ledge
if he doesn't take the cold plunge.

The boys' father shouts, "My dad
brought us here every summer,
to this same swimming hole,
and nothing bad happened!"

After a few false starts,
the boy plugs his nose, closes his eyes,
then jumps. His scream echoes
downward, as if this is the last sound
he'll ever make.

For the rest of the day, three brothers
take turns climbing the hill to the train tracks
and diving into the still waters below.

Sunburned and laughing, they stop
at the general store for sodas.
Shocked by their story of trestle jumping,
the proprietor says, "Are you crazy?
They rebuilt that bridge a decade ago
after the old trestle collapsed into the river.
No one ever extracted the scrap heap,
so it still lurks under the water."

Everyone laughs because no one
was impaled on the rusted skeleton
and they are all somehow still alive.

People Only Remember the Burning

Crumbling lumber and two arid years of drought
        reduce the old barn to kindling,
patiently awaiting a rogue spark.
        Autumn leaves reflect the shimmering
red and yellow hues that sway with the flames.
        Significance of the crumbling structure
dissipates in smoke as a new history settles
        in the ashes of town folklore, a cautionary tale
of three delinquent boys
        trying to make an impression
on girls with reputations. Those local boys
        who smoke Marlboros and drink stolen cans of Coors.
Those truant boys raze a local landmark to the ground.
        Everyone knows those boys are trouble.
The next morning, the local newspaper omits
        the names of the minors involved in the incident.

        Other omissions were made;
        most of the news story was wrong,
        and hearsay stained the actual events.
                There were no girls
                in the barn that night.
        We smoked Camels.
        The cans of Coors weren't ours.
                They belonged to our fathers
                who drank and worked for hours
        on the broken-down Ford truck
        that would never run.
                Pulsating Sabbath and Skynyrd
                and smashing beer bottles
                on a Friday night
        drove us out of the house
        to the old barn.
                Jack dropped
                his pocket knife.

He couldn't relax
without the blade in his palm
    since the nightly altercations
    with both parents
    escalated to bruises.
    Even sleep wasn't safe anymore.

Batteries dead in the flashlight,
Sam lit a match to look for the blade.

    In the dark,
    we smelled smoke,

    saw the flames

    and we ran.

        We're still running.

        Some things refuse
        to burn down.

Learning How to Drown

I.

Traffic lights flash slow yellow
over intersections where no one

crosses paths this close to midnight.
Yield in every direction. Spirits drift

under fluorescent lamps
in the vacant Walmart parking lot,

but if you look close enough,
it's just August air thick with humidity.

Most households are turned down for the night
as I cross Harrison Avenue and Miller Street.

Police cruiser clocks me,
running my plates for priors

or outstanding warrants, analyzing my driving
for signs of intoxication.

Their message is clear,
I am not supposed to be here.

Anyone on the streets at this hour
is suspect somehow.

Thread the needle of driving
under the speed limit but not slow enough

to make my avoidance apparent. No rolling
stops at stop signs, I give the bored patrol

no reason to pull me over and find
the weed in the glove compartment.

Mine is an inverted existence
where night is day and day is night,

working third shift as a temp at the plastics factory
for the summer. Time and my place in it

isn't clear or linear. I am a tourist
wandering through lives in progress.

In a few weeks, I will be gone,
barely a fuzzy blip to anyone.

This is why no one bothers
to learn my name.

II.

Most of the skeleton crew
look exhausted

before the shift starts. Still,
we have eight mind-numbing hours ahead.

The brittle thin couple, Amy and Jim,
are androgynous, interchangeable.

They could pass
for twin mannequins

except they move and speak.
They are already tweaking

and fidgeting. Most nights,
they crash before lunch.

We form a crescent moon
around Bill, our mumbling shift manager,

who appears as wrinkled and threadbare
as his faded flannel shirt.

If Dr. Jekyll had kept a menagerie
of Mr. Hydes under his skin

and they took turns on the carousel
of his consciousness, this would be Bill.

There are as many versions of him
as there are brands of booze

or varieties of narcotics.
Tonight, it is 'Pills Bill'

who appears when we clock in
then disappears until dawn.

What reaction is justified after you reach
the arduous peak of your life

only to realize you were scaling
a mountain of garbage?

All of this is according to employees
who mock Bill,

gossip in the parking lot,
and snicker as he calls out

who will work each press for the night.
There is no winning or losing,

all of the machines are equally
tedious and soul-erasing.

Each decrepit press is kept on life support
well beyond its intended lifespan.

They labor heavily as if running in place
with a collapsed lung.

As each machine gives up the ghost,
an alarm rings

like a heartbeat flatlining on a monitor.
With each mechanical breakdown,

a voice that sounds like a refrigerator
thrown down a flight of stairs

erupts in a stream of obscenities.
You can hear the fury of a life wasted

patching together so many things
that want to stay broken,

machines or otherwise.
Watching that fucking boulder

roll down the same goddamn hill
again and again.

Todd, the third-shift mechanic, is a balding,
grease-covered, speed-addled,

ball of rage menacing the factory floor
like a schoolyard bully in steel-toed boots.

The ever-present wrench in his white-knuckled fist
always looks like a weapon.

Each press is an unwilling Lazarus
          dragged back to life night after night.

Less a savior, Todd is more of a masochist.
          If the machines could feel anything,

they would have a shared sense of impermanence
          with those of us who occupy the assembly lines.

III.

All summer, humans and machines produce
          cheap promotional plastic products

for an animated movie no one will remember,
          sold at a burger chain

that will declare bankruptcy in the coming years.
          Everything we make is garbage

and now overflows landfills.
          "Anyway, it's a paycheck," Candy says,

"Who gives a shit where this junk goes?"
          Someone is going to make it,

and it might as well be her.
          She is behind on bills,

and her car needs a catalytic converter.
          And they don't do drug screenings,

which is an invasion of fucking privacy,
          by the way, she reminds me frequently.

What she does in her free time
          is none of their goddamn business.

She walks out to Kyla's Ford Focus
            where they smoke meth during lunch.

Alone in my Mercury Comet,
            I eat a bologna sandwich and spark a joint.

The sun will rise in a few hours. I will
            be gone in the coming weeks,

back to state college, a blue-collar, free-lunch,
            food-stamps kid who sells plasma

twice a week to pay for textbooks
            and works at factories

over breaks to pay tuition. For this entire
            exhausting summer, I have been

misplaced in the world, like a lighthouse
            in a landlocked town.

Inside the other parked cars,
            cigarette cherries glow red

in the dark. Smoke rolls out of the windows.
            Pale faces gaze into the night.

Small embers pulse
            with each deep inhalation,

thinking about whatever other people think about
            at three in the morning, alone in their car,

when August heat
            doesn't relent even at night,

just like everything else that stalks
at the dark edges

of the yellow street light,
seeking one moment of turbulent peace

before heading back
into the belly of the rusted beast.

IV.

At four in the morning, time contorts.
Early morning hours elongate

like taffy sagging in the middle as it stretches.
Mixed with moderate insobriety,

the monotonous sound of the machines
becomes a rhythm that dulls anyone

between waking dream
and sleepwalking reality.

Operating a press for hours is muscle memory,
rhythm, and timing, nothing to do with skill.

Close the metal door, open the metal door,
pull out eight hot plastic cups,

place them in a box, close the door, open the door,
hot plastic cups, stack in boxes,

open, cups, box, close, open, cups,
box, close, open, cups, box, close, open,

cups, box, close, open, cups, box, close,
open, cups, box, close, open, cups, box, close

open, cups, box, close, open, cups, box, close,
    open, cups, box, close, open, cups, box, close, open,

cups, box, close, open, cups, box, close, open, cups, box,
    close, open, cups, box, close.

Urban legend says that if you disturb a sleepwalker
    mid-dream, they would be shocked awake

and suffer a heart attack. This is not true.
    Otherwise, we would all be casualties

scattered across the factory floor when the bell rings
    at the end of our shift every night.

We walk fatigued out of the building. Jolted
    by sunrise, fresh air that isn't toxic,

and a rush of nicotine from the first drag
    off the first cigarette in hours.

Cicadas are already stirring up
    their low morning hum

that swells to a deafening assault
    in the afternoon. As scheduled, their brood

returned after seventeen years.
    Staring through her thick sunglasses,

Candy says, "Jesus Christ, has it been seventeen years?
    I started working at this fucking place last time

those disgusting bugs covered everything.
    I was a temp worker like you."

During the summer of the previous Brood X,
	Kyla married that cheating piece of shit, Rick.

"That was a great summer," she says,
	"nothing like this one."

V.

In unison, a dozen cars pull out of the factory.
	The Walmart parking lot

no longer looks haunted. Daylight exchanges
	one kind of ghost for another.

No cops follow me home.
	They are perched

under overpasses hunting
	for speeders on the interstate.

I smoke one last joint before pulling up
	to the duplex rental across from the county jail.

I meet my father at the front door,
	his figure framed, like gazing into a mirror,

one that reflects a future waiting at the far end
	of a road long-rutted with hardship

and the gravel of regret.
	He nods and says there is still coffee

as he heads out for first shift
	at the driveshaft factory.

Rinse off and lie down, I listen
	to the rattle of the electric gate

across the street, open and close as cops
          exchange shifts.

Wake mid-afternoon in a haze, unsure
          if it is morning or evening. All summer,

I exist outside of time and inside a future
          that is already waiting,

all I have to do is nothing
          and it is ready to begin.

Like learning how to drown;
          just stop treading water,

don't panic, as the surface
          disappears.

Or choose to swim until I lose sight
          of the shore, until I have no choice

but to keep swimming
          out into the bottomless dark.

Distance to Here

Two letters in the fluorescent grocery store sign
        flicker on the verge of burning out.
A cracked display window held together
        with masking tape and last week's sales circular
resembles a belated birthday gift
        from a distant, alcoholic relative.
Craters in the maroon stucco
        look like the pockmarked surface of Mars.

Two decades ago,
        the facade facelift was fresh.
New automatic doors swung wide
        as if welcoming the future with a rush
of frigid conditioned air
        and the mineral smell of fresh asphalt.
We were bag boys collecting shopping carts
        in the parking lot. Too stoned to care
about these jobs or this town. Our futures
        were yellow brick roads
laid ahead of us in golden promise.
        We were confident that they destined us
anywhere but here. One night after our shift,
        we made a wager in that parking lot to see
who would move the farthest fastest.
        Your sights were set on Seattle.

We never noticed
        the funeral home across the street
where I stand now. Neither
        of our younger selves would ever believe
this is where the future ends.
        Distance from there and then
to here and now is a stunted fifty yards.

Place a mask over my face,
        guide myself by the hand into your wake,

back into the unrelenting present
        where you now reside in my past.
Mourners stay arm's length away.
        We grieve your short life, your long death.
Your breath held for years,
        as you waited for the future to start
until you chose to stop
        waiting and breathing.

No Face Charlie

After late summer sundown, Route 351 is quiet except
for crickets chirping in the dark. When the wind
makes the trees whisper, those are my favorite evenings.
Rustling leaves sound like so many things. Often, the ocean

comes to mind. I've never seen it. It's nowhere near here,
yet I hear it in the trees. Even if my eyes worked,
it wouldn't matter. There is nothing to see except
the stars on a clear night, but I remember

what those twinkling pinpoints look like.
My feet read the ground like braille. It's not difficult
to tell the difference between smooth blacktop
and crunchy gravel. I wouldn't get run over

because cars announce their presence miles before
they arrive. This Doppler effect gives me plenty of time
to hide behind the textured trunks of black oak trees.
Minding their own business, those folks on their way

to Youngstown don't need a terrible fright
at the sight of my face in their headlights. The morning
of the bird's nest under Morado Bridge, forty years ago,
outside of Beaver Falls, is a blur. My friends said

I wanted to count the eggs and sort out their species,
which sounds like something I would do. I climbed up
the steel girders like so many maple trees in summer.
Near the nest, my friends said sparks burst like fireworks.

My rag-doll body was tossed twenty yards.
I hit the ground like a sack of bloody potatoes.
When folks ask, *Why didn't you see the power line?*
I have no answer. I don't remember. I guess I am fortunate

in some way because I also don't know what it feels like
to have twenty thousand volts surge through my limbs,
burn out my eyes, melt my face, and stop my heart.
Folks ask, *What was it like to be dead?* I hate

disappointing them, but there wasn't anything.
Sometimes, I say there was a bright light. This white lie
eases their mind, and that's fine with me. According
to the Post Gazette, I was supposed to die like Robert Littell—

another twelve-year-old who touched that wire
beneath Morado Bridge. He died instantly. I woke
disoriented in a black room with no doors, swallowed
by pain. Doctors told me I was lucky to be alive.

My little sister was the first to scream when she saw me,
but I would get used to that reaction. I felt terrible
for scaring her and giving her nightmares. It took years
for her to be in the same room with me.

I walk after dark to not scare children or cause panic.
This is not the only reason I hide behind trees when cars approach.
There have been men with abrasive voices and bellowing laughter
who threw me in the ditch, teenagers with eggs and toilet paper,

or women laughing. I could feel their long fingers pointing.
But most folks are polite. After turning off their engine,
I recognize a friendly voice when they call my name.
Six summers ago, a car pulled up, and a woman asked

if I needed a ride. She gasped when she saw my face.
She said she would walk with me if that was OK.
Her name was Claire. She would pass by on her way home
from working second shift at the local switchboard. New to town,

new to her tedious job and newly divorced, she didn't know anyone,
they didn't know her, and she liked it that way. We walked
my isolated patch of road a dozen times in the relentless heat
of late summer. She used to live near Lake Superior, where the air

always has a chill, even in August. She didn't stop by every day.
Then one day, she stopped driving this way altogether. I don't know
what happened. I never heard from her again. I didn't tell anyone
about Claire and now wonder if she was real. No one from town

mentioned a stranger moving in and then out. I don't need anyone
telling me she would never fall in love with me. I already know that.
More than once, Claire mentioned wanting to live near the ocean.
I like to think she is somewhere on the shore watching

the tide. I can almost hear it. Maybe she will take a road trip to visit
her folks in Chicago. Her new husband drives as he listens
to the ball game on the radio. She looks out the window, recognizes
the passing landscape, and remembers that displaced summer

after her divorce. On the map sprawled across her lap,
she spots Route 351. Maybe she wonders if that disfigured man
still strolls at night. Sometimes, I imagine she is in the car,
passing by, as I hide behind the rough bark of a black oak tree.

How Ghosts are Born

A narrow tunnel of headlights
guides me down
this two-lane state road
on the outskirts of Youngstown.
A shadow breaks free
of the dark and darts
from the shoulder,
flattens under the tire.

On the side of the road,
darkness thick as an oil spill.
The cracked grill of the car
wheezes like an asthma attack.
On the shore of my high beams,
I see the limp paw of a tan dog.
Under its mouth is a spark,
a dull name tag, engraving erased,
rendering the body
a John or Jane Doe.

Silhouette of three distant houses
in the moonlight.
I can't go from door to door
in the middle of the night.
No other choice but drive away,
leaving the warm body
steaming where it lies.

I convince myself
that this dog's owners
never travel this stretch of road.
They tell their children
animals get lost all the time
but friendly folks take in strays.
Their lost dog is happy
with a new family.

Repeat a lie long enough
until it feels plausible.

Not knowing what happened
is a scar that stays a mystery,
cataloged in their collective narrative,
where everyone swears
when the house is quiet and dark,
they still hear scratching
at the back porch door
years later.

Books by Joseph Kerschbaum

Learning How to Drown
Midnight Sunrise
Mirror Box
Distant Shores of a Split Second
Ken: a man for all seasons
Your Casual Survival
The Handless Long for Sign Language
Dead Stars Have No Graves
The Composer Steps into the Fire
The Human Remains

Joseph Kerschbaum is the author of ten poetry collections and two spoken word albums. His most recent books include *Midnight Sunrise, Mirror Box,* and *Distant Shores of a Split Second.*

Joseph has performed at venues and festivals across the United States, captivating audiences with his dynamic and emotionally resonant performances. He was the captain of the Bloomington Poetry Slam and has competed in the Midwest Poetry Slam League. Joseph also toured extensively with The Reservoir Dogwoods, a collective of four Indiana-based poets known for their high-energy readings and poetic camaraderie.

Joseph is the recipient of a Greer Foundation Fellowship for Creative Writing from the Bloomington Area Arts Council, which supported the completion of his collection *Dead Stars Have No Graves.* He has also received an Individual Artist Grant from the Indiana Arts Commission and the National Endowment for the Arts.

His work has appeared in numerous journals and magazines, including *Street Cake Magazine, The Dallas Review, Heimat Review, Wild Roof Journal, Trampoline, Hamilton Stone Review,* and *Reed Magazine.* He has been nominated for both the Pushcart Prize and Best of the Net.

Joseph lives in Bloomington, Indiana, with his family, where he continues to write, perform, and support the literary arts.

www.ingramcontent.com/pod-product-compliance
Lightning Source LLC
LaVergne TN
LVHW090542110826
845146LV00003B/1226

* 9 7 9 8 8 9 9 9 0 3 6 3 2 *